D0712578

School Jokes

Why did the caterpillar go to the library?

It wanted to become a bookworm.

COMPILED BY PAM ROSENBERG • ILLUSTRATED BY BOB OSTROM

Special thanks to Katie Cottrell for her
assistance in compiling source materials.

Published by The Child's World®
1980 Lookout Drive • Mankato, MN 56003-1705
800-599-READ • www.childsworld.com

Acknowledgments
The Child's World®: Mary Berendes, Publishing Director
The Design Lab: Design
Jody Jensen Shaffer: Editing

ISBN 9781623239992
LCCN 2013947279

Printed in the United States of America
Mankato, MN
November, 2013
PA02196

Where do young cows eat at school?
In the calf-eteria.

Why did the computer go to the school cafeteria?
It wanted a few bytes.

What happened to the vegetables that were misbehaving in the school cafeteria?
They found themselves in hot water.

Why did the cafeteria worker wear Rollerblades?

So she could serve fast food.

LANGUAGE ARTS JOKES

Why did the mailman take the alphabet?
So he could deliver the letters.

What do you get if you cross the alphabet with a spinning top?
Dizzy spells.

What do you get when you cross the English department with the school cafeteria?
Alphabet soup.

MOM: My child is a genius. She has the most original ideas, hasn't she?
TEACHER: Yes, especially when it comes to spelling.

What happened when the English teacher's dictionary was stolen?
She was at a loss for words.
What happened to the student who swallowed the dictionary?
The school nurse couldn't get a word out of him.
What do elves learn in school?
The elf-abet.
ABC

What did the pig put in the school computer?
Sloppy disks.

Why did the cat take a computer class?

It wanted to get hold of a mouse.

AT THE LIBRARY
Why did the caterpillar go to the library?
It wanted to become a bookworm.
Who guards the school library? The bookkeeper.

MISCELLANEOUS JOKES

Why did the third grader bring a lightbulb to school?
She had a bright idea.

Did you hear about the cross-eyed teacher?
She couldn't control her pupils.

What do you get when you cross a goat with a kangaroo?
A kid with a built-in schoolbag.

Why did the guitar leave music class?
Everyone kept picking on it.

What would you get if you crossed a vampire and a teacher?
Lots of blood tests.

Why did the kids get wet going to school?
They were in a car pool.

Why did members of the drama club get sent to detention?

They kept acting up.

Knock Knock.
Who's there?
Don Juan.
Don Juan who?
Don Juan to go to school today.

What's yellow, has wheels, and lies on its back?

A dead school bus.

Why did the student bring a ladder to school?

She was interested in higher education.

Is your teacher strict?

I don't know. I'm too scared to ask.

TEACHER: You missed school yesterday, didn't you?
PUPIL: Not very much!

TEACHER: Does anyone know which month has 28 days in it?
RUSSELL: All of them.

TEACHER: Why are you writing on a piece of sandpaper?
SARAH: You told us to write a rough draft.

SALLY: My teacher doesn't even know what a horse looks like.
MOM: That's impossible.
SALLY: Well, I drew a picture of a horse and she asked me what it was.

PUPIL (ON PHONE): My son has a bad cold and won't be able to come to school today.
SCHOOL SECRETARY: Who is this?
PUPIL: This is my father speaking.

HOMEWORK, TEST, AND REPORT CARD JOKES

What grades did the pirate get in school?
High seas.

Is it better to do your home-work on a full stomach or an empty stomach?
It's better to do it on paper.

What happened when the sailor saw his report card?
He got C sick.

Why did the student glue himself to his report?
He was trying to stick to the subject.

SALLY: I don't think I deserve a zero on this test.
MOM: Neither do I, but it's the lowest mark I can think of.

TEACHER: Where is your homework?
JAKE: I lost it fighting this kid who said you weren't the best teacher in school!

MOM: Sit down and show me your report card.
SON: I can't sit down. I just showed it to Dad.

What can you never make with poor penmanship?
Straight As.

TEACHER: I take real pleasure in giving you a 90 on this test.
MATT: Then why don't you give me a 100 and really enjoy yourself?

GIRL MONSTER: Mommy, the teacher said I was neat, pretty, and well behaved.
MOMMY MONSTER: Don't worry, dear. You'll do better next time.

Why did the D student take his report card to the beach?
He wanted to get it above C level.

TEACHER: You copied from Katie's exam paper, didn't you?
MATT: How did you know?
Teacher: Katie's paper says, "I don't know," and your paper says, "Me neither!"
TEACHER: This test is multiple choice.
JOSEPH: Then I choose not to take it!
What kind of tests do witches take at school?
Hex-aminations.
Why was the little bird punished?
It was caught peeping during a test.

THE PRINCIPAL'S OFFICE

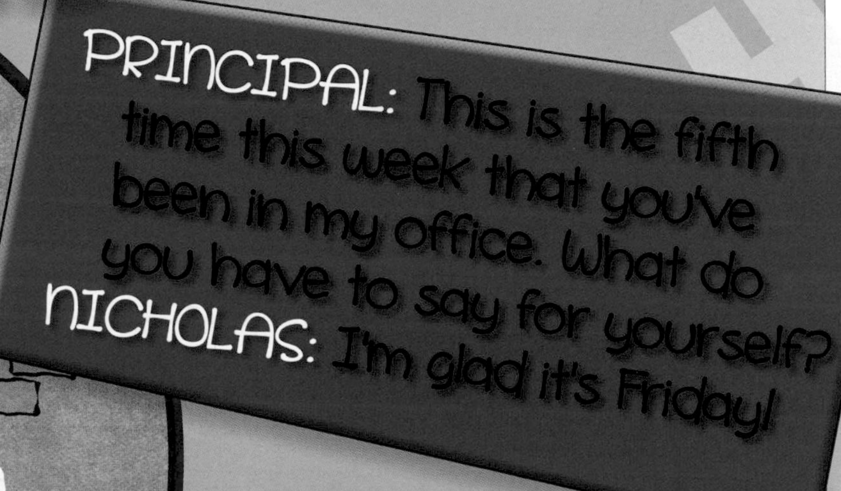

TEACHER: I'm having trouble with one of my students.
PRINCIPAL: What's the problem?
TEACHER: Not only is he the worst-behaved child in class, he has a perfect attendance record.

What would you get if you crossed an English teacher with the track team?
A run-on sentence.

Why was the music teacher so good at baseball?
She had perfect pitch.

Why did the tiny ghost join the football team?
He heard they could use a little school spirit.

Why couldn't the elephant join the swim team?
He forgot his trunks.

Why did the doughnut join the basketball team?
To practice dunking.

Why did the basketball player start a fire?
The coach told him to warm the bench.

Why did the locomotive go to the gym?
It wanted to join the track team.
STUDENT: The doctor says I can't play football.
COACH: I could have told you that.
12
7
15

TRADE SCHOOL

Is a hammer a useful tool in math?

No, but multi-pliers are.

Why did the electrician go to school?

To study current events.

What did the builder do his homework on?

Construction paper.

Why did the carpenter study math?
4 x4 16
x1
2 x2 84
3 x3 9
So he could make multiplication tables.
What did the carpenter make for the textbook? A table of contents.

MATH JOKES

If you cut 2 apples and 3 pears into 10 pieces each, what would you have?
Fruit salad.

If you had 200 pennies, 100 nickels, and 75 quarters in your pockets, what would you have?
Droopy pants.

How do you recognize math plants?
They have square roots.

What do math teachers wear to ballet class?
Two-twos.

What would you have if you had five apples in one hand and three in the other?
Huge hands.

Why is 3 + 3 = 7 like your left foot?
Because it's not right.

TEACHER: Now, class, whenever I ask, I want you to all answer at once. How much is five plus four?
CLASS: All at once!
PATRICK: Mom, can you help me find the lowest common denominator in this problem?
MOM: Don't tell me they haven't found it yet. They were looking for it when I was in school!
MATH TEACHER: What is a polygon?
STUDENT: A dead parrot.
What kind of food do math teachers like?
Square meals.

SOCIAL STUDIES JOKES

What are the small rivers that run into the Nile?
The juve-niles.

TEACHER: What's the difference between an American student and an English student?
STUDENT: About 3,000 miles.

TEACHER: Why does the Statue of Liberty stand in New York Harbor?
JUDI: Because it can't sit down.

Why did the history book go out so much?
It had a lot of dates.

DAD: Why aren't you doing well in history?
DANIEL: Because the teacher keeps asking about things that happened before I was born!

What do you call the first page of a geography book?
The table of continents.

GEOGRAPHY TEACHER:
What's the most slippery
country in the world?
STUDENT: Greece.
MAP
HISTORY TEACHER:
When was the
Great Depression?
STUDENT: The last
time I got my
report card.
GEOGRAPHY TEACHER:
What has two humps and
is found at the North Pole?
STUDENT: A lost camel.

SCIENCE JOKES

Why did the baby go to chemistry class?
To learn formulas.

What would you get if you crossed the geology department with the school band?

Rock music.

SCIENCE TEACHER: Why do birds fly south in the winter?
STUDENT: Because it's too far to walk.

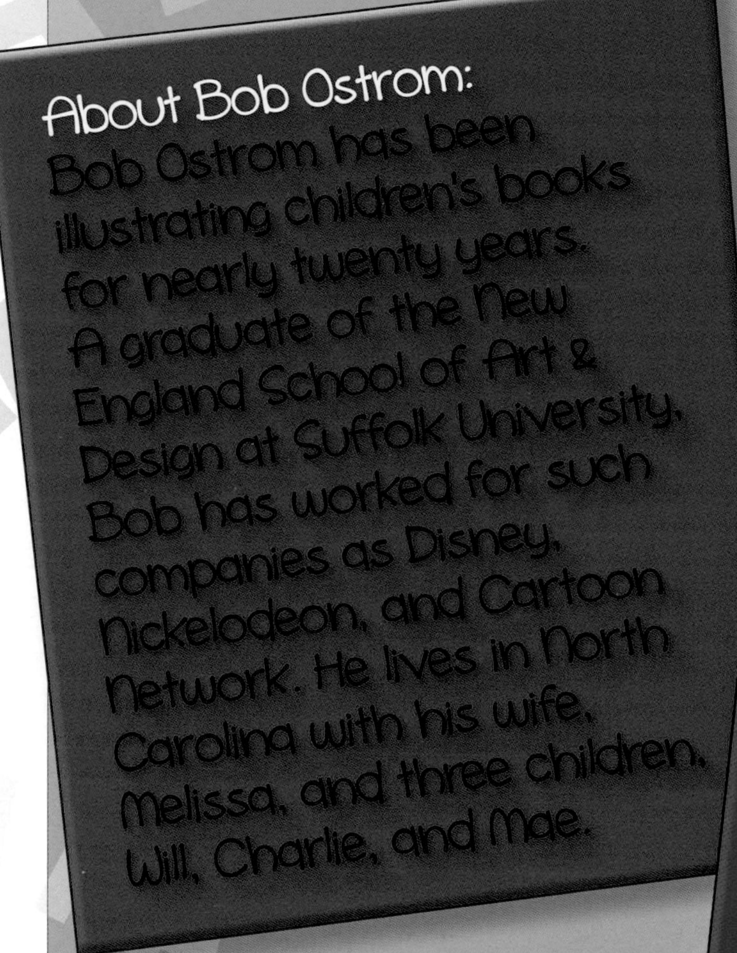

About Pam Rosenberg:

Pam Rosenberg is a former junior high school teacher and corporate trainer. She currently works as a author, editor, and the mother of Sarah and Jake. She took on this project as a service to all her fellow parents of young children. At least now their kids will have lots of jokes to choose from when looking for the one they will tell their parents over and over and over again!